Digging for Goals

A Breakthrough Approach to Becoming Your Best Self

By Mary Barnes Johnson

Balboa Press books may be ordered through booksellers or by contacting:

Balboa Press
A Division of Hay House
1663 Liberty Drive
Bloomington, IN 47403
www.balboapress.com
1 (877) 407-4847

ISBN: 978-1-5043-4731-0 (sc)
ISBN: 978-1-5043-4732-7 (e)

Library of Congress Control Number: 2015921287

Print information available on the last page.

Balboa Press rev. date: 02/15/2016

BALBOA
PRESS
A DIVISION OF HAY HOUSE

To everyone who has been by my side as a teacher
of my "life lessons" or as a fellow student, I thank you.

—MARY

"At times our own light goes out and is rekindled by a spark from another person. Each of
us has cause to think with deep gratitude of those who have lighted the flame within us."

—ALBERT SCHWEITZER

Table of Contents

Acknowledgments

To my husband Fred—thank you for believing in me. Your unconditional love, daily laughter, thoughtful honesty, and sincere encouragement are gifts for which I am very grateful. I knew that from the moment we met, there were angels amongst us. We are truly blessed and I thank you for helping to make my dreams a reality.

To Mom and Dad—thank you for giving me life. I miss you both and am proud to be your daughter. My level of appreciation for the life lessons that you taught me knows no boundaries.

To my family—I appreciate you for the unique gifts you bring to make us a family, and admire the individuality that define you as your true "self." I continue to learn so much from all of you. Thank you.

To my friends and colleagues—thank you for being so supportive and encouraging in all facets of my life. I am a better person because you have been my friends, my mentors, and my teammates. You know who you are and my immense gratitude is sprinkled with love and respect.

To Richard Kessler—living proof of what goal setting can do! I am forever grateful for the opportunity Kesslers provided. Working hand-in-hand with such amazing people is a gift I will always treasure.

To Bill Aberman—thank you for encouraging me to grow, to honor myself, and to trust my intuition. The quote you shared below by Shel Silverstein spoke to my heart immediately, and I will follow it all the days of my life.

To Roy Williams—thank you for founding Wizard Academy! It is a magical place that inspires me to color outside of the lines and stretch myself creatively, spiritually and academically.

"Listen to the mustn'ts, child. Listen to the don'ts. Listen to the shouldn'ts, the impossibles, the won'ts. Listen to the never haves, then listen close to me… Anything can happen, child. Anything can be."

—Shel Silverstein

Foreword

Sometimes, when I am talking to someone about a goal he or she wants to accomplish, he or she will comment, "that sounds hard!" I remind them, "With all due respect, it is only hard—not impossible. Most things in life that are truly worthwhile are hard. Can you do hard things?"

The process of identifying a goal, setting a course, taking action toward the achievement, and sustaining that progress on into your future is a daunting task. It is not surprising that so many feel frustrated because what they wanted to accomplish never came to be.

In a culture that looks for simple answers to complex questions, **Digging for Goals** stands out as an in-depth look at the real process of making your life's desires come to fruition. There are multiple dimensions to achieving a goal that you set. It requires clear vision, decisive action, emotional strength, and the ability to overcome obstacles. This can seem to be a daunting path. Some will look at what is necessary and give up before even starting the process. But for those who are ready to make the commitment and do the work that is required, it is possible to acquire the skills to set your own path and make your goal a reality.

In **Digging for Goals**, Mary Barnes Johnson takes you on a journey of learning. She helps you to identify what you will need for this endeavor and gives you the tools to acquire the skills that are essential in making progress toward your goals. She then provides you with the clarity of understanding how to make this accomplishment a fixture of your life going forward.

Can you do hard things?

That is the question posed to the readers of this book. Important accomplishments are hard. That is not an excuse. If you are willing to do hard things, Mary Barnes Johnson, through this book, will help you to walk, step by step, to make your goals a reality. I hope you will accompany her on this journey.

— John Weaver, Psy.D.
Author of *The Prevention of Depression: A Missing Piece in Wellness* and *The Healthy Thinking Program Training Manual.*

Introduction

"A dream is just a dream. A GOAL is a DREAM with a PLAN and a DEADLINE."

— HARVEY MACKAY

 *Could you be doing better and achieving more?*

 *Do you lack a sense of direction or purpose?*

 *Are you frustrated or overwhelmed?*

If you answered "YES" to any of these questions, then ***Digging for Goals*** is for you!

I want to personally congratulate you for having the courage to take the first step in determining what you need to get from "here" to "there" in your life. Whether you want to take steps to secure your financial future, improve your relationships, change careers, build a stronger alliance with your teams, de-clutter your home environment, find your "happy" again, embrace a healthy lifestyle or just eliminate stress from your day, ***Digging for Goals*** will help you to acheive that!

Every day, successful people work toward making their dreams a reality. They take the time to create a vision in great detail as to what they want any given area of their life to look like. They look at the obstacles that could get in the way, and put plans in place to prepare them for when the obstacle appears. Successful people also make time to revisit their goal on a regular basis to chart their progress and "imagine" how it will feel when they have accomplished it.

I have read hundreds of books on topics involving Leadership, Sales, Coaching and Self-help. The 35 years I have spent in the jewelry industry gifted me with opportunities to work with individuals in determining and achieving their goals. ***Digging for Goals*** is a user-friendly workbook designed to help you and your teams turn dreams into reality.

Diamonds are multi-faceted, and so are you. ***Digging for Goals*** will help you to determine your level of satisfaction in various "facets" or areas of your life, and help you to decide where you would like to see improvement. The Wheel of Life Exercise will enable you to look inside these facets, thus making it easier for you to decide what facet you want to start polishing! Don't worry about making the wrong decision—worry about making no decision at all!

Digging for Goals is designed to help you to:

- Imagine a brighter future
- Commit to a plan
- Uncover obstacles
- Stay Motivated
- Chart your progress
- Revisit your goal
- Celebrate your success!

Procrastinating about your dreams won't make them go away.

As the immortal Arthur Ashe once said:

"Start where you are. Use what you have. Do what you can".

What better way to begin this journey?

"Trust yourself. Create the kind of self that you will be happy to live with all of your life. Make the most of yourself by fanning the tiny, inner sparks of possibility into the flames of achievement."

—Golda Meir

Charting Your Course

This is important in the goal-setting process because it requires planning and projecting a realistic view of the journey ahead. Look for potential obstacles that may come across your path and devise a variety of solutions that will resolve the setback and get you back on track.

What things will get in your way? Fear, excuses, and outside obstacles.

Fear of:

Failure	Success	Intimacy
Rejection	Being alone	Risk-taking
Change	Technology	Commitment

Digging for Goals provides you with tools to help you recognize and conquer unhealthy fear. With practice, you will find the exercises in the first five chapters to be healthy techniques that aid in addressing and moving past fear. In addition to these practices, seeking coaching or therapy is another valuable resource to better understand yourself and overcome your fears.

Fear can be a good thing because it can alert us of danger. Fear can affirm us when our intuition is telling us to do things a certain way. Fear can keep us safe. This is a healthy fear.

There is another face to fear, and the one I am referring to is fear that keeps us right where we are. The fear of making a change…the kind of fear that paralyzes. The fear that gets in the way of you being able to set goals and follow them through to the end. This is an unhealthy fear.

How can you deal with fear?
1. Name it
2. Categorize it as healthy or unhealthy
3. Transform or reframe it
4. Let it go

By giving the fear a name, it is easier to describe and determine if it is really true, and whether it is a healthy or unhealthy fear. The practice of reframing fear helps to put it in perspective. Be honest with yourself and be prepared to handle the obstacle. When it arrives, deal with it and let it go.

When you stop feeding fear, excuses, and obstacles that get in your way, you take back your control, your time, and your energy. You regain clarity and can move forward. The better prepared you are to address these, the more successful you will be at accomplishing those important things that you want in your life.

Chapter

I

"The secret of change is to focus all of your energy,
not on fighting the old, but on building the new."

—SOCRATES

Living The
Four Daily Practices:

Journaling

Gratitude

Self-discipline

Forgiveness

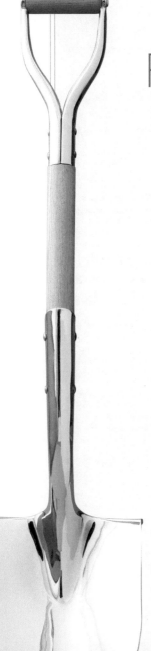

On Journaling...

What is the benefit of writing thoughts in a journal?

People that journal show improvements in self-esteem and life satisfaction within the first few weeks of keeping journals. One of the values of journaling is that it slows down the thinking process. This leads to greater clarity of thought, thus providing better guidance in making good decisions that support efforts to accomplish your goal. Journaling develops your level of observation, which helps you to get through difficult times more quickly. Keeping a journal is a tool to track your progress toward your goal, and when you see progress, self-motivation will remain high.

Why should I do it?

1. Journaling helps people to feel more optimistic, more connected to others, and those who journal describe feeling in a better mood.

2. According to a study at Massachusetts General Hospital, journaling has helped veterans who have suffered from post-traumatic stress get through difficult times more quickly.

3. Journaling reported higher levels of positive emotions, life satisfaction, vitality and optimism according to a study at the University of California at Davis. The same study reported that journaling lowered levels of depression and stress.

4. In a study at The University of Rochester Medical Center, it was determined that keeping a journal can help you discover the triggers that cause stress and anxiety. Once identified you can work on a plan to resolve the problems and, in turn, reduce stress.

5. University of Texas at Austin psychologist and researcher James Pennebaker believes that writing about stressful events helps you come to terms with them, thus reducing the impact of these stressors on your physical health.

How do I get started?

Answer the following questions to begin your journal entry:

- *What went well today?*
- *What didn't go so well?*
- *How could I have handled it differently?*
- *What am I grateful for?*
- *What is my intention for tomorrow?*

"Happiness doesn't depend on any external conditions, it is governed by our mental attitude."

—Dale Carnegie

Gratitude

Gratitude is a combination of thanks and appreciation for what a person receives, whether tangible or intangible. With gratitude, people acknowledge the goodness in their lives.

Are you willing to try a little experiment?

1. Point to yourself.
2. Look at where you are pointing.

Most likely, you are pointing to your heart. Why? Because we instinctively feel the heart is the essence of who we are. Most of us consider the heart to be the core of our emotions. Our hearts are the center of human happiness and wisdom.

Dr. Robert A. Emmons of the University of California, Davis and Dr. Michael E. McCullough of the University of Miami have done much research on gratitude. Studies published on this topic determine that when we fill our hearts with gratitude, loving kindness, appreciation, openness and forgiveness, we increase the production of good hormones. Research has shown that after 10 weeks of practicing gratitude through writing, creative visualization, positive affirmations, or visually seeking positive actions in others, people experience these things:

- Feel more positive emotions
- Relish good experiences
- Improve health
- Exercise more
- Deal with adversity
- Build stronger relationships

How often do we make time to write notes and letters to people for whom we are grateful when they come to mind? What stops us from picking up the phone to verbally deliver a message of thanks, admiration, or gratitude? How come we don't take the time to pay these people a visit to let them know how they impacted our lives? Oftentimes, we put them off until the day comes when you get that email or phone call from an old acquaintance with an obituary announcement. The obituary is for someone that you always enjoyed, appreciated, admired, looked up to and now they are gone. You rearrange your schedule, call the florist, and make time to "get away" in order to tell the people that are alive how you felt about the deceased. Is there anyone else who finds this disturbing?

The technique of letter writing is the quickest way to shift moods according to research conducted by Martin Seligman, Ph.D. The importance of developing a positive mood (by being more grateful) is that it opens your mind to more possibilities rather then remaining narrowly focused. When unexpected obstacles occur during your goal-setting process, you will be better equipped to form a new strategy and move forward with a renewed motivation towards staying on track to accomplish your goal.

If maintaining relationships with someone is a goal of yours, then perhaps you can see how action steps such as making a weekly phone call, sending a card, writing

> "Gratitude is not only the greatest of virtues, but the parent of all others."
>
> —CICERO

an email, or scheduling a date or visit can keep this goal in the forefront. You may be addressing a potential obstacle such as "time management" by working these steps into your calendar. The reward of accomplishing these action steps is the joy and connectedness you feel by demonstrating appreciation for them and just how important they are to you. That's gratitude at its finest.

> *How would you feel if you received a card or letter from someone that thanked you for being you?*
>
> *How would that impact you?*
>
> *What would it encourage you to do?*

Research has also shown that practicing gratitude can have a positive impact on self-motivation, which is a necessary tool in goal-setting.

What are you waiting for?

Self-Discipline

Decision-making and discipline together make a great marriage for success.

Goal-setting requires you to make a decision, but if you don't have the discipline to follow through with the action steps and accountability, you won't reach the goal. On the flip side, if all you have is discipline without a decision, life can feel very regimented without much gratification.

So, by making a great decision about an area of your life (Your Value-Driven Goal), and weaving discipline into the plan (Commitment to the Action Steps and Overcoming Obstacles), you create a strong fabric in which you can proudly wear for the rest of your life (Your Character).

How can you develop discipline?

1. Make a daily "to-do" list and prioritize it. What is of most importance and how much time do you need to finish it? Start at the top, document the time of completion and get to work on your list. When you clear out the old, you make room for something new.

2. Stop listening to and/or believing the excuses that you have been telling yourself. Instead, look for evidence to dispute negative beliefs. Develop constructive inner dialogue that is deliberate and productive.

3. Recognize "triggers" and determine how to deal with them. Part of "mastering your feelings" is learning to identify your obstacle and implement a healthy solution to overcome it. Change unlocks from the inside and you hold the key.

Reward yourself when you are finished…not "almost" done.

> "The will to succeed is important, but what is more important is the will to prepare."
>
> —BOBBY KNIGHT

What are some common mistakes people make that reflect a lack of discipline?

According to time management expert Donald E. Wetmore, there are common mistakes people make regularly that keep them from performing at their best. The ones I have chosen to list here are:

1. **Clutter:** Clutter can really play havoc on your mental attitude and can escalate feelings of being overwhelmed. So much that you may quit before you even attempt to try! "Studies have shown that the person who works with a messy desk spends, on average, one-and-a-half hours per day looking for things or being distracted by things," Whetmore says. "That's seven-and-a-half hours per week!"

2. **Starting the day without a plan:** Time management helps make the most of your time. The benefits of multi-tasking are a myth with a lot of research to stand behind that. Studies show that we frequently overestimate our ability to handle multiple tasks. For early humans, that sort of miscalculation could have meant becoming a lion's lunch! Today, the consequences of multi-tasking are most likely to show up as stress, a mistake, or maybe even a car crash.

3. **Working through lunch:** Even a 15-minute break will charge up your batteries. After doing what we do for several hours, we start to dull out and lose motivation and concentration. A break will clear your head and aid in effectively handling the afternoon challenges.

4. **Believing excuses:** Excuses pull you away from your goal and grant you permission to quit. By eliminating excuses and accepting responsibility for your life, you find ways to move through, over or around obstacles while keeping your eye on the end result.

Forgiveness

One of the first and most important steps in the goal-setting process: take responsibility for your "Self".

Self-forgiveness is not easy, but it is well worth the effort! Forgiving yourself is a process that takes courage, compassion and self-love. It takes courage to re-open an emotional wound that is harboring guilt, shame, embarrassment, anger or self-criticism. It requires compassion to acknowledge the pain and feel a sense of remorse. Self-love enables your to take responsibility for your actions and move forward in the process of self-forgiveness.

You are not the only one who has made mistakes…everyone makes them. They can range in size from small mishaps to major crimes and a whole lot of mistakes fall in-between those bookends. Whatever you can take ownership of and feel some remorse toward is a mistake you can begin to forgive yourself for. This journey may not be easy, but it is achievable. When it happens, it will result in a feeling of relief. By forgiving yourself, you acknowledge that you want to make a change in your life and it encourages the ability to learn from your mistakes. When you mindfully affirm the change that you want to have happen (The Goal), and identify the challenges that you previously ignored (The Obstacles), you are more likely to take full responsibility of the outcome (The Action Steps). Forgiveness helps you to get past those "old tapes" that might be making you feel stuck or afraid.

Acknowledge your mistakes, forgive yourself, apply the lesson learned and grant yourself permission to create the life that you want!

Forgiving others is also difficult because the pain you feel from someone's betrayal or hurtful behavior can breed feelings of bitterness and hard-heartedness. As you replay the incident, the anger and resentment keep you connected to the past. Your thoughts keep the hurt and/or "back stabbing" alive, which can harbor revenge making it a lot more difficult to move ahead. You remain feeling stuck. Long story short, the stress caused by carrying around these feelings is really unhealthy. According to a research study directed by Dr. Luskin, a Palo Alto psychologist and author of "Forgive for Good: A Proven Prescription for Health and Happiness" the benefits are as follows:

- 27% reduction in physical symptoms of stress, such as backache, headache, sleeplessness and upset stomach
- 42% decrease in depression
- 62% decrease in feelings of hurt
- 15% reduction in long-term feelings of anger
- 35% increase in self-confidence

Forgiving reduces stress and improves your health physically, mentally, emotionally, and spiritually. Most importantly, forgiving someone is not saying that what they did to you is okay. Forgiving someone is saying that you choose not to carry that toxic burden of anger inside you anymore. Being angry only hurts you…not the person who did the action. Love yourself enough to let go of the anger and replace that

> "As long as you don't forgive, who and whatever it is will occupy a rent-free space in your mind."
>
> —Isabelle Holland

space with something healthy that invigorates you, fills you up, and motivates you to keep moving forward toward your goal.

- *How does **un-forgiveness** serve you?*
- *What does it feel like?*
- *How could you release those feelings?*
- *What could be different?*
- *What does **forgiveness** look like?*
- *What happens inside when you forgive?*
- *What can you learn from it?*
- *How can that impact you moving forward?*

"If you can't
forgive
and forget,
pick one."

—ROBERT BRAULT

Chapter

2

"Most folks are as happy as they make up their minds to be."

—Abraham Lincoln

Assessing
Your Wheel Of Life

Let's get started!

The purpose behind doing this first exercise is to give you a visual breakdown of the areas in your life. By taking the time to list the individual areas and rate your present level of satisfaction in each, you will discover a visual "snapshot" of where you are today.

Oftentimes, this exercise will help to determine where you want to start making changes in your life.

Health/Physical: Consider level of fitness, nutrition, weight, energy, quality of sleep, dental hygiene, yearly exams, etc. How do you take care of yourself?

Home Environment: Consider your home…how cluttered or clean is it? How well do you like the décor and the colors? How well do you like the neighborhood? How does your home affect your sense of well-being and fulfillment?

Family/Friends: How satisfied are you with the friendships and relationships that you have? Do they contribute to an overall sense of happiness? Do they make you a better person? Can you imagine areas that could be improved?

Spiritual/Personal Growth: How satisfied are you with the choices you have made to stretch and grow? What do you do to learn, improve, or stretch yourself?

Significant Other or Romance: How satisfied are you with the relationship that you have or that you don't have?

Career: Consider your career selection, your current job responsibilities, and the direction you want to take. Consider your work environment as it pertains to your sense of well-being and fulfillment.

Financial: Consider income, savings, retirement planning, and your overall spending and investment habits. How satisfied are you with your financial future?

Play/Fun: Consider what re-creates your energy and rejuvenates your spirit. Consider how often you employ these activities…how often do you make time for them?

The eight sections represent "Life Balance."

Now, with the center of the wheel being "0" and the outer edge being a "10", list your present level of satisfaction in each section with a number and a line. To illustrate:

- A ten would be "completely satisfied with this section and all is good. No changes needed here."
- A five would be "okay, but changes could make it much better in the long run."
- A zero would mean "no satisfaction or fulfillment whatsoever. Everything could use a change."

(See an example on the lower right corner of the next page.)

"Respect for ourselves guides our morals; Respect for others guides our manners."

—LAWRENCE STERNE

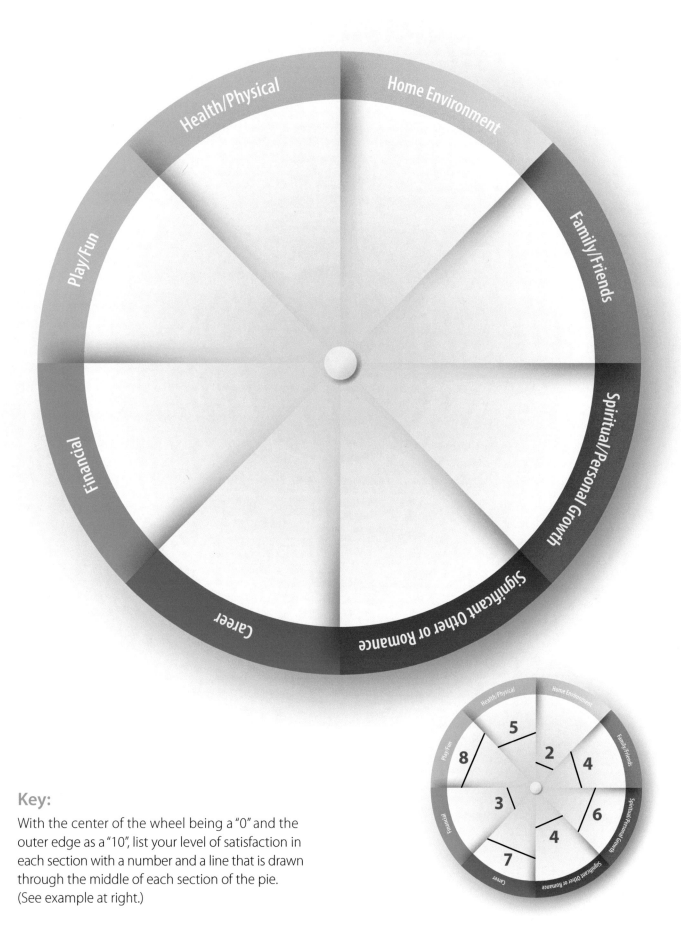

Key:

With the center of the wheel being a "0" and the outer edge as a "10", list your level of satisfaction in each section with a number and a line that is drawn through the middle of each section of the pie. (See example at right.)

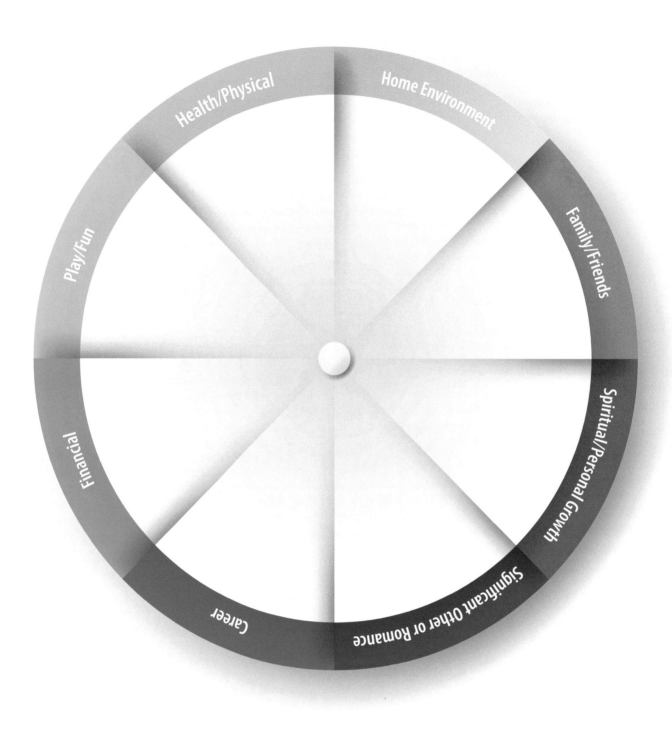

Transfer your scores to this page to make answering the following questions easier.

This circle represents your "Wheel of Life."

Does it look bumpy? If it does—that's OK. It's to be expected. Answering the 14 questions below will help you to understand how you script your day, your life, and your personal satisfaction with each.

1. Which section do you spend the majority of your time?

   _____

2. Which section do you invest the most of your money?

   _____

3. Which section do you invest the most of your energy?

   _____

4. Which section causes you the most stress?

   _____

5. Which section is the most important to you?

   _____

6. Which section gives you the most energy?

   _____

7. Which section depletes you of energy?

   _____

8. What section provides you with the most support?

   _____

9. What section is the least supportive?

   _____

10. What section is the most challenging for you?

    _____

11. Which section do you take the most pride in?

    _____

12. What section are you most motivated to work on?

    _____

13. How would raising that number impact the other sections of your wheel?

    _____

14. How would you score your level of satisfaction with your life overall?

    _____

> "Progress is impossible without change, and those who can not change their minds can not change anything."
>
> —George Bernard Shaw

Chapter

3

"Open your arms to change, but don't let go of your values."

—Dalai Lama

Connecting
With Your Values

"Too often we underestimate the power of a touch, a smile, a kind word, a listening ear, an honest compliment, or the smallest act of caring, all of which have the potential to turn life around."

—LEO BUSCAGLIA

The Difference Between
Values & Beliefs

What five things do you **love** about yourself?

Recognizing what your values are is a key component in determining your goals. For clarification, it is important to understand the difference between <u>values</u> and <u>beliefs</u>.

Values are the fabric of who we are as individuals. Our values give us meaning and a sense of identity. Values are the basis for our behavior, our motivation, and define what we desire or seek to achieve. In other words, the stronger our behavior reflects the values that we imply to hold, the more strongly we actually hold that value. Values govern our behaviors and motivations, therefore, our perceptions of reality. By aligning your goals with your values, motivation will naturally increase, as does your commitment to your goal. When we neglect our values and worry over life's unavoidable obstacles, we lose our sense of direction. Our self-esteem takes a big hit and we lose focus on who we are.

Beliefs are judgments or generalizations that reflect how we view both our "self" and the world around us. Beliefs shape your reality, and can influence behaviors and thoughts in very powerful ways. Beliefs give our experiences meaning, and will affect our behaviors and attitudes towards people and situations.

The list you are about to create is your core value list. Keep this handy as you prepare to set goals. By listing goals that are aligned with your core values, the process will be better understood and positive results will more likely be achieved.

When we make a conscious decision to live by our core values, we feel better because we are in harmony with ourselves.

Determining Your Core Values

Knowing your values will help you to create a life that is more satisfying and meaningful. You will discover what inspires you, what you enjoy, what you feel is important, and what you would like to see more of.

This list is designed to give you some sample values, and assist you in thinking of what is uniquely important to **YOU**.

Setting goals is a lot easier when you determine what values are of most importance to you. Give some thought to the following questions as you look over the list. Highlight the top ten values and feel free to add other values that may not be listed!

Accomplishment	Enthusiasm	Order
Accuracy	Entrepreneurship	Participation
Achievement	Excellence	Partnership
Acknowledgment	Fairness	Passion
Advancement	Fame	Patience
Adventure	Flexibility	Peace
Advocacy	Focus	Politeness
Affection	Forgiveness	Presence
Authenticity	Free Choice	Respect
Balance	Fun	Recognition
Beauty	Generosity	Resourcefulness
Boldness	Gentleness	Romance
Calm	Growth	Safety
Caring	Happiness	Security
Challenge	Health	Service
Cheerfulness	Honesty	Self-Esteem
Collaboration	Individualism	Self-Reliance
Companionship	Independence	Simplicity
Compassion	Integrity	Spontaneity
Confidence	Innovation	Strength
Contentment	Intuition	Tact
Cooperation	Joy	Thankfulness
Courage	Kindness	Tolerance
Creativity	Learning	Travel
Curiosity	Leisure	Trust
Dependability	Listening	Understanding
Determination	Love	Volunteerism
Discovery	Loyalty	Wisdom
Education	Optimism	Others???

Did you know that when you react with anger or disgust toward a person or a situation, it is often because that person or incident is actually stepping on a core value of yours? If your goal and your values are in alignment, your brain will do everything in its power to overcome hurdles and obstacles, to keep you moving toward your goal throughout the day.

Now you have looked over the list of values—and perhaps have come up with some of your own. Answer the following questions to gain insight into your core values.

1. Which of these values speak to you?

   _____

2. Which values strike your heart?

   _____

3. Which of these values represent what you truly care about?

   _____

4. How are you practicing, promoting, and living these values?

   _____

5. Which of these values represent that which is important to you?

   _____

6. What is challenging about practicing, promoting, and living these values?

   _____

7. Which values can't you live without?

   _____

8. Which values do you admire in people?

   _____

9. When making your most important decisions, what fundamental values do you base them on?

   _____

The list you have created is your core value list. Keep it nearby as you continue to dig deeper into the goal setting process.

Chapter

4

"All of our dreams can come true
if we have the courage to pursue them."

—WALT DISNEY

Practicing
Creative Visualization

Creative Visualization Exercise

What is "Creative Visualization"? Creative visualization is a version of *healthy daydreaming*. It is the technique of using your imagination or visual mental imagery to picture specific behaviors, things, or events that you want to occur in your life. It is to purposefully engage all of your senses and see the image as though it is your reality. Many people prefer to close their eyes, but your eyes can remain open.

Why would you practice this? **Because it works**!! Athletes such as Tiger Woods and Michael Jordan frequently use Creative Visualization to enhance their performance in sports. A gymnast that performs on the balance beam will mentally visualize and replay each and every movement that they make in their routine. Sales professionals will visually role-play the greeting, seating, meeting and handshake of the sale made prior to meeting with clients.

Who has benefited from this practice? Actors such as Will Smith, Oprah, and Jim Carrey have encouraged Creative Visualization to overcome obstacles and to imagine success. In fact, in an interview with Oprah in 1997, Jim Carrey told the audience that he wrote a check to himself for 10 million dollars and added the notation, "for acting services rendered." Within ten years, Jim Carrey did indeed receive $10M for his role in "Dumb and Dumber".

How do you creatively visualize? Imagination and childlike daydreams are a great place to start. Create or imagine in great detail what you desire and then visualize it over and over again with all of the senses (i.e., What do you see? What do you feel? What do you hear? What does it smell like?)

Where do I begin? Determine your goal…what do you aspire to be? What do you want to acquire or accomplish? What would you like to improve?

1. Get into a comfortable position and **close your eyes**.

2. **Inhale** through your nose for a '3' second count.

3. **Exhale** through your nose for a '6' second count.

   —Continue this breath-work through out the exercise—

4. **Picture tension leaving** your body through toes, fingertips, and ears.

5. Let your inner voice **count backwards** from **10–1**.

6. **Imagine** the thing you want **in great detail** as though you have it **NOW**.

7. **Enjoy** the image for three minutes **engaging all of your senses**.

8. Mentally **move** the image to a **place** that is **accessible** for the next time.

9. Open your eyes and **write it down with as much detail as possible**.

10. Verbally **affirm** what you wrote down.

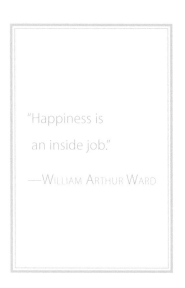

"Happiness is
an inside job."
—WILLIAM ARTHUR WARD

So, if you can make 3–5 minutes available per day, you are adding another very effective tool to making your dreams a reality! Creative Visualization will absolutely help to make your goals crystal clear and enable you to "taste the flavor" of achieving them!

Describe in great detail what you visualized in your exercise.

_____

_____

_____

_____

_____

_____

_____

_____

_____

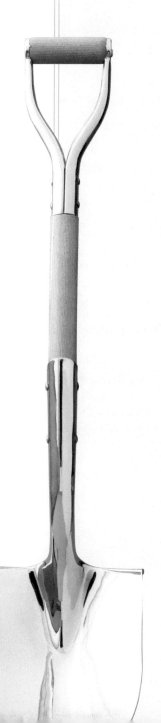

Chapter

5

"Nothing is impossible. The word itself says, 'I'm Possible!'"

—AUDREY HEPBURN

Using Positive Affirmations

Positive Affirmation Exercise

What are positive affirmations? Verbal or written phrases repeated (or meditated on) to program the subconscious mind and bring about the desired outcome you seek in the goal-setting process.

Why would you practice this? Positive Affirmations help to clear the clutter of negative mind chatter and the feelings of despair. Positive affirmations help turn "wishful thinking" into **action** and **results**.

Who has benefited from this practice? Helen Keller and Winston Churchill, along with Mahatma Gandhi, Dr. Wayne Dyer and many others. According to songwriter/musician Willie Nelson, "Once you start replacing negative thoughts with positive ones, you will start having positive results."

How do you find the words? Make a mantra or an affirmation your own…use words that resonate with you. It can be simple and short, or very specific. Your choice!

Where do I begin?

1. Phrase affirmations **in the present tense**…not in the future.

   "I am a fit 150lb runner enjoying my training schedule as I prepare for my first 5k."

2. Always affirm **what you DO want**…not what you DON'T want.

   "I am financially secure and all my monetary needs are met."

3. Make is **short and simple**.

   "I see it, believe it, and feel I can achieve it."

4. Always choose an affirmation or mantra that **feels totally right for YOU**.

   "I am the GREATEST!" Muhammad Ali believed this and believed that if he said it enough, he would convince the world that he was the greatest.

5. Affirmations are meant to help you to **create a new point of view**.

When repeating affirmations upon awakening or right before you sleep, you have the best access to your subconscious. You are actually retraining your brain by reprogramming your self-image to see yourself as you want to be. As you set your goals and imagine yourself achieving them, the words you speak or think impact your life. You manifest what you believe. Choose to be positive as this contributes to your overall success in goal-setting and turning your dreams into reality.

"All that we are is a result of all that we thought."

—BUDDA

"If you can imagine it, you can achieve it. If you can dream it, you can become it."

—WILLIAM ARTHUR WARD

Record your affirmations here.

_____
_____
_____
_____
_____
_____
_____
_____
_____
_____
_____
_____
_____
_____
_____
_____
_____
_____
_____
_____
_____
_____
_____
_____
_____
_____
_____
_____

"Your world is a living expression of how you are using and have used your mind."

—EARL NIGHTINGALE

The benefits of using positive thoughts and words:

Researchers at the University of Scranton, PA, discovered that people who have the most success achieving their goals are those who are fully willing and ready to commit to a change. They were not just aware of their desires; they embraced **specific tools** and **strategies** that challenged the way they thought, viewed, and behaved in the world. Positive thinking (**Creative Visualization**) and positive self-talk (**Positive Affirmations**) are tools for **building self-esteem and self-worth**. The most successful individuals in the study were those who consciously chose to reinforce their affirmations and new behaviors on a daily basis.

The more positive thoughts, feelings and words you choose to use throughout the day, the more success you will generate in every facet of your life. These positive thoughts create positive energy, which helps to keep people motivated during their goal-setting journey.

The benefits of saying it "out loud:"

By telling as many people as you can about your goal, it increases your level of accountability as well as motivation necessary for stick-to-it-ness.

People who successfully maintained their commitment to achieving their goals for longer then six months **made use of their social networks** to include family, friends, colleagues, and organized groups. Rallying others around your goal helps you to stay committed. Partnering up with someone who is looking to accomplish a similar goal has great benefits. Joint workouts, cheering each other on and holding one another to a level of accountability are all wonderful ways to stay motivated.

The benefits of "seeing" your goal in all its glory:

By creating a **"Vision Board"** or a "Vision Notebook", you get a crystal clear picture of your journey since choosing your goal. This tool helps to support your goals and dreams and should be a collage of the things you desire and commit to achieving. Use pictures from travel and fitness magazines, write your personal affirmations and be creative in expressing how you feel and what you desire. Look at all eight areas from your Wheel of Life exercise and imagine what a "10" would look like in each section. Get others involved in the excitement and make a point to look at it daily, as it will help keep you focused on the end-result…YOU!!!

"Good habits are as addictive as bad habits, and a lot more rewarding."

—Harvey MacKay

Chapter

6

"To succeed, you need to find something to hold on to,
something to motivate you, and something to inspire you"

—TONY DORSETT

Apply Your Favorite
Goal-Setting Approach

Dig Deep

Like diamonds, human beings are unique and fall into different learning styles. ***Digging for Goals*** honors these differences by providing seven examples of goal-setting…appropriately named after diamond shapes!

Take a look at the seven goal-setting samples that appear on the following pages. As you familiarize yourself with them, keep this in mind:

- Each of the seven samples offers one goal-setting approach.
- Each goal-setting approach has two sections:
  - The first section helps you clarify your goals;
  - The second section is where you write your goals down.
- Select the sample that most resonates with you.
- Commit to what you have written and accomplish your goal!

The more specific you can be with your goals, the easier it will be to remember them, commit to them, and accomplish them.

"When we long for life without difficulties, remind us that oaks grow strong in contrary winds and diamonds are made under pressure."

—Peter Marshall

"You must take personal responsibility. You cannot change the circumstances, the seasons or the wind. but you can change yourself. That is something you have charge of."

—Jim Rohn

Goal-Setting Example

Here is an example of what goal-setting looks like from start to finish.

GOAL: I will increase my household income by $3,000 by 12/31.

Each goal will ask for two or three action steps.

1. ACTION STEP: *I will take my lunch to work every day.* *(Weekly savings – $40)*

2. ACTION STEP: *I will eliminate my morning latte' purchase.* *(Weekly savings – $15)*

3. ACTION STEP: *I will ride-share to my job 2x/week.* *(Weekly savings – $10)*

✓ **Your total projected savings over 50 weeks: $3,250!**

There will be obstacles. What are some? Be honest with yourself!

1. OBSTACLE: *Not making the time to pack my lunch in the morning.*

2. OBSTACLE: *My head says I need my morning latte' fix.*

3. OBSTACLE: *Sharing transportation seems like a hassle.*

How can you prepare to overcome the obstacle when it presents itself?

1. SOLUTION: *Pack my lunch the night before.*

2. SOLUTION: *Make my coffee drink at home.*

3. SOLUTION: *Use the "share" time for pleasure or work-related reading.*

How can you monitor your accountability, and track your progress?

1. TRACKING: *Create a spreadsheet reflecting your weekly savings.*

2. ACCOUNTABILITY: *Deposit the money saved into a separate account.*

How will you celebrate your accomplished goal?

Congratulations! I will use 10% of the money I saved to treat myself.

Did you notice that none of the action steps involved getting a monetary raise? Choose action steps that you have control over. Anything extra is a bonus!

> "Don't let the fear of striking out hold you back."
>
> —BABE RUTH

Dig Deep:
The Round Brilliant Approach

Section 1: Clarify your goals.

Self:

- Are you happy with the choices you've made that put you here and now?
- Do you like who you are?
- Base all of your decisions NOW on the person that you would like to become.

Career:

- Are you a part of the solution or part of the problem in your workplace?
- Do you do the minimum requirement or purposefully leave your workplace better then when you arrived?

Family:

- Whatever your role is… do you take responsibility for your position?

Friend:

On being a friend to someone: What does that look like to you?

- Look at the circle of friends you have chosen. Are they right for you?
- How do your friendships make you a better person?

Spirituality and Personal Growth:

- How are you stretching yourself to grow, to learn, and to reach?
- Are you fulfilled within the spiritual community that you have chosen?
- How can you be at peace with yourself and the world around you?

Health:

- Are you treating your "gift of life" with respect and care?

Section 2: Write your goals down.

Specific goal with date to accomplish it by:

1. _____
2. _____
3. _____

Action steps to take in order to accomplish each goal:

1. _____
2. _____
3. _____

1. _____
2. _____
3. _____

1. _____
2. _____
3. _____

What do I fear could happen to lose my motivation?

1. _____
2. _____
3. _____

The new strategy I will use to get me back on track:

1. _____
2. _____
3. _____

How will I keep track of my progress toward reaching my goals?

1. _____
2. _____
3. _____

How will I feel and celebrate the accomplishment of each goal?

1. _____
2. _____
3. _____

Dig Deep:
The Radiant Approach

Section 1: Clarify your goals.

It is all about making choices. What can you do to get from "here" to "there"?

- **Educate yourself:** How could you do that?
- **Try your best:** What does "best" look like to you?
- **Risk failure:** What is the worst thing that could happen?
- **Take a chance:** What are you afraid of?
- **Learn from others:** What are those who are respected and successful doing?
- **Develop self-discipline:** What could you do more of? Less of?
- **Visualize your success:** Close your eyes…what do you see?
- **Raise your bar:** What might happen if you did?
- **Be brave:** What would that feel like?

This is not a formula…it is a choice. It is a decision that you make because you want to improve yourself and your life. It is a "new attitude"… a philosophy that you create, embrace, and live by. It aligns with your values. Look at the areas of your life that you want to improve.

How important is this goal to **you** on a scale from 1–10?

- What is getting in your way?
- Does this goal align with your values?
- How does this goal fit with your priorities and lifestyle?
- How does this goal impact other areas of your life?

Imagine that you have reached your goal…

- What is it like?
- Where are you?
- What does it feel like?
- What do you see?
- What do you hear?
- What are you telling yourself?

Make your goal-setting journey fun and successful! It's all up to you!

Section 2: Write your goals down.

My goals in detail with a completion date:

1. _____
2. _____
3. _____

I commit to doing these two things for each of my goals:

1. _____
2. _____

1. _____
2. _____

1. _____
2. _____

The obstacles that could sabotage my goals are:

1. _____
2. _____
3. _____

I will deal with the obstacles in this way:

1. _____
2. _____
3. _____

I will celebrate and reward my success in accomplishing my goals by:

_____
_____
_____

Dig Deep:
The Emerald Approach

Section 1: Clarify your goals.

What are Goals?

Simply put, goals are the things that you want to do, to be, or to have in your life.

Why is the "goal setting format" necessary?

The format provides the "map" and you are the expert in creating this roadmap in your life. Since goals are uniquely your own, it is imperative that the goal resonates with you. Without something to focus on, the decisions that we make and the actions that we take will likely have no long-term attachment to our future. Without the long-term thinking, you could waste a lot of time driving aimlessly on the road to "Nowhere" and arrive in the land of "Missed Opportunities!"

What is the importance of putting it on paper?

Writing goals on a piece of paper allows you to "see" **what** it is that you want to accomplish in life and **how** you are going to do that. The value of writing is to establish **in your own words** the goals that give your life meaning, direction, and a sense of purpose. With these things comes a sense of personal responsibility and self-control, which will also make you feel happier inside and more empowered. You will learn to steer your life in the direction that you want it to go, rather then taking just any road that intersects with the one you are on. By writing your action steps you are committing to the "plan". When documenting potential obstacles and setbacks, you are preparing yourself to deal with them instead of being taken by surprise. Being in control of this helps you to stay on track rather then getting derailed on your journey.

That can't be too hard…what's the catch?

Here's the irony. A lot of people invest money in books, seminars and academic institutions to study, read, and learn how to be successful yet never apply what they have learned. What's the point of learning it if you don't apply it? The truth of the matter is that your brain has a tendency to sabotage your plan. Think about it…it took a lot of neural energy overtime to build all of your bad habits and your brain isn't necessarily excited about the idea of change! It's comfortable in its complacent or sedentary state and staying put is just fine with your mind. The good news is that you can change your mind! The voice in your head that says, "Don't bother" has to be silenced by the voice that is screaming out "DO IT!" By applying the "positive" kind of verbiage (Positive Affirmations) with the "positive" kind of thinking (Creative Visualization) and the "positive" kinds of activities (Vision Boards, Journaling and Meditation), you can stimulate the motivational centers of your brain to create satisfaction and success as you see it! **You can do this!**

Section 2: Write your goal down.

What do I want?

1. _____
2. _____
3. _____

How will I get there?

1. _____
2. _____

1. _____
2. _____

1. _____
2. _____

What is standing in my way?

1. _____
2. _____
3. _____

How can I "look it in the eye" and move past it instead of it stopping me?

1. _____
2. _____
3. _____

How can I measure my progress to know I am on track?

1. _____
2. _____
3. _____

How am I going to know when I have accomplished my goal?

1. _____
2. _____
3. _____

How am I going to celebrate my accomplishments?

_____
_____

Dig Deep: The Pear Approach

Section 1: Clarify your goals.

Setting the Goal:

Take time to ask yourself these questions:

- What is it that I really want?
- What specific outcome am I looking for?
- If I could change anything, what would it be?
- What one thing do I never want to bother with again?
- What do I want improved?

Moving from "goal setting" to "goal getting:"

- What steps can I take to make this goal a reality?
- Which of these steps can I start acting on right now?
- Why do I want to accomplish this goal?
- How will my life be different when I accomplish this goal?
- How can I make this more fun as I move closer to my goal?

Make it S.M.A.R.T.

- **Specific:**
  Make this a well thought out goal with detailed clarity so you know exactly what you are trying to achieve.
- **Measureable:**
  Something that can be tracked in $$$, practice, time and number so you can track your progress and know when you have accomplished your goal!
- **Authentic:**
  Is it aligned with your values and vision? Does it feel "right"?
- **Realistic:**
  In the big picture, is it achievable and something you really want?
- **Tangible:**
  Is it a solid, concrete goal that is specific, measurable, authentic, realistic and worth celebrating when you have arrived at it?

Section 2: Write your goals down.

Specific goals:

1. _____
2. _____
3. _____

Measurable action steps:

1. _____
2. _____

1. _____
2. _____

1. _____
2. _____

Authentic tools to keep me motivated:

1. _____
2. _____
3. _____

Realistic obstacles that may arise:

1. _____
2. _____
3. _____

How I will celebrate my success:

1. _____
2. _____
3. _____

Dig Deep:
The Marquise Approach

Section 1: Clarify your goals.

How does this apply to me?

If you were told that you are the "epitome" of a friend, a spouse, a son or daughter, a parent, a colleague, a leader, or a volunteer, what would that look like to you? How would those who felt you possessed the most ideal and essential qualities describe you? What qualities and courtesies would you demonstrate in order to be viewed and admired as such? How would you be described by your family, your extended family, and by your community?

What are my resources?

Take a look inside yourself, than seek the counsel of other successful people that you respect and look up to. If you were to ask those people what has really helped them get where they are in life, invariably they will talk about a dream, a goal, a mission, or a purpose. They would describe something that has been motivating them throughout the years to stay "attached" to their long-term vision. Most likely, it will align with their values and their vision is crystal clear.

Where do I begin?

S Select your goals
U Understand your plan of action
C Creatively visualize your goals
C Commit to your goal-setting process
E Expect problems to occur
S Stand firm on your original commitment to the goals you set
S Stretch yourself to success

When we **take responsibility** for our own personal happiness and success, we realize that we can indeed become happier. We grow through both joy and pain, and the end result is personal achievement. We develop potential when we accept personal responsibility.

Section 2: Write your goals down.

What are my goals?

1. _____

2. _____

3. _____

What can I commit to so I am on the road to success?

1. _____

2. _____

1. _____

2. _____

1. _____

2. _____

How will I hold myself accountable and on track?

1. _____

2. _____

3. _____

What can get in the way of my success?

1. _____

2. _____

3. _____

How will I put the obstacles aside and stay on course?

1. _____

2. _____

3. _____

When I accomplish these goals, how will I reflect and celebrate the triumph?

_____

_____

_____

Dig Deep:
The Heart Approach

Section 1: Clarify your goals.

Where will you be one year from today?

How will you get there?

Do you know the three most common errors people make in goal setting?

1. They don't write them down and put them in plain view to revisit daily.

2. They don't make a plan to achieve their goal.

3. They don't commit or live up to the commitments they make.

If you have found yourself looking back on goals unachieved, don't despair! You can overcome the obstacles and accomplish what you want to!

Never limit your potential and don't sell yourself short.

Here's how in five steps:

1. **Identify it:** Write your goals down clearly. Write down exactly what you want to achieve in the most specific terms possible.

2. **Date it:** Put a date and a time limit to start the goal and finish it. If you do not commit to a start and target an end, your ability to achieve your goals is questionable.

3. **List the obstacles:** What are those saboteurs, those naysayers, and the inevitable setbacks that could stand in your way? Identifying obstacles helps prevent them from occurring.

4. **Write down an action plan for each goal:** Will you need help from others? Do you need to acquire new skills and knowledge to get you from "here" to "there"? Will you need to reschedule your morning or evening routine?

5. **List the benefits of achieving your goal:** What's in it for you? What is your incentive and is it strong enough to ensure achievement? How will it make you feel when you can say, **"I DID IT!"**

Goal achievement is up to you…your self-talk (Positive Affirmations and Journaling), self-imagination (Creative Visualization and Vision Board), and self-determination (Practicing Gratitude and Self-Motivation) are 90% of the achievement process.

What is standing in your way?

Section 2: Write your goals down.

I will be/have _____ by _____/_____/_____

    1. _____

    2. _____

    3. _____

I will succeed by implementing these steps:

    1. _____

    2. _____

    3. _____

    1. _____

    2. _____

    3. _____

    1. _____

    2. _____

    3. _____

The obstacles that I may face during this time are:

    1. _____

    2. _____

    3. _____

I overcome those obstacles by doing this:

    1. _____

    2. _____

    3. _____

I hold myself accountable by tracking my progress in this way:

    1. _____

    2. _____

    3. _____

In celebration of saying "I DID IT", I will reward myself by:

    1. _____

    2. _____

    3. _____

Dig Deep:
The Oval Approach

Section 1: Clarify your goals.

Goals are statements of what you want to do. In essence: **The Written Word**.

Does goal setting really work?

Yes! Goal setting is a powerful exercise. When you write down your plans in crystal clear detail and imagine them as though they are already present, you create a healthy environment to breed success. Commitment and clarity make a unified team to support you in turning your plans into reality.

What's the purpose? What's the process?

Since the purpose of setting goals is to move you forward and spur positive change, the process of setting goals allows you to choose how you are going to get there. Goal setting propels forward motion. What might previously have seemed like a long and arduous journey suddenly looks and feels like an attainable trek.

Goal setting provides long-term vision that helps to:
- Improve performance
- Increase your pride and satisfaction
- Increase your motivation to achieve
- Improve your self-confidence
- Eliminate the attitudes that hold you back (negative self-talk)

Is it easy to do?

It is not always easy to reach goals, but the benefits of sticking to the plan are hugely rewarding. The one thing to remember is that you must consider what you are willing to change to reach your goal. "You can have anything, but not everything" is a quote I have often repeated. If you have the goal of losing weight, you may choose smaller portion sizes or recalculate the number of calories necessary to accommodate your lifestyle change. You may have to redesign some social happy hour time in order to incorporate exercise into your schedule. On the flip side, you can create new opportunities by spearheading a walking group at noon, a weekly recipe exchange, or design a "wellness challenge" at the workplace or at home. Think of how the people you spend time with and your current environment can be helpful towards you reaching your goals. Easy? Not always, but you can be creative and have fun!

Section 2: Write your goals down.

My three most important goals are:

1. _____
2. _____
3. _____

The steps I will implement to meet my goals are:

1. _____
2. _____

1. _____
2. _____

1. _____
2. _____

The obstacles that could get in my way are:

1. _____
2. _____
3. _____

The things that will help me to stick to my goals are:

1. _____
2. _____
3. _____

The deadline I have set to accomplish my goals is:

1. _____
2. _____
3. _____

I will track my progress and know I have achieved my goals when:

1. _____
2. _____
3. _____

I will celebrate my accomplishment by:

_____
_____

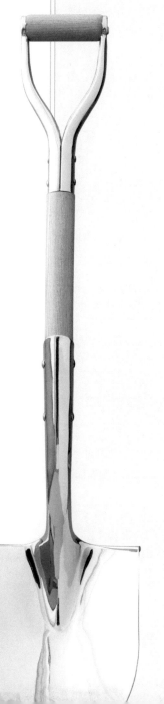

Chapter

7

"Making the decision to start puts us on our path
to success; discipline helps us to cross our finish line."

—Mary Barnes Johnson

Journaling
For Maximizing
Your Goals

Journal Pages

Write & Reflect

Journaling accesses both sides of your brain and this makes it a great tool for staying motivated throughout your goal-setting process. While your analytical and rational left-brain is busy with the act of writing, your right-brain is given permission to feel and tune-in to what's going on. Journaling will help you to uncover obstacles and create possibilities as you move forward towards achieving your goal. This is YOUR journal and the more honest and open you are in your writing, the better you will understand yourself and the world around you.

Suggested questions to start with:

- What went well today?
- What didn't go so well?
- How could I have handled it differently?
- What "stirred" inside?
- What am I grateful for?
- What is my intention for tomorrow?

_____

_____

_____

_____

_____

_____

_____

_____

_____

_____

_____

_____

_____

_____

_____

_____

_____

_____

_____

_____

_____

_____

_____

_____

_____

_____

_____

_____

_____

_____

_____

_____

_____

_____

_____

_____

_____

_____

_____

_____

"Your beliefs become your thoughts, your thoughts become your words, your words become your actions, your actions become your habits, your habits become your values, your values become your destiny."

—MAHATMAN GANDHI

"Giving up on your goal because of one setback, is like

slashing your other three tires because you got one flat."

—Anonymous

_____
_____
_____
_____
_____
_____
_____
_____
_____
_____
_____
_____
_____
_____
_____
_____
_____
_____
_____
_____
_____
_____
_____
_____

_____
_____
_____
_____
_____
_____
_____
_____
_____
_____
_____
_____
_____
_____
_____
_____
_____
_____
_____
_____
_____
_____
_____
_____
_____

"I have seen the best of you and the worst of you and I choose both."

—Sarah Kay

"If your dreams don't scare you, they are not big enough."

—Ellen Johnson Sirleaf

_____
_____
_____
_____
_____
_____
_____
_____
_____
_____
_____
_____
_____
_____
_____
_____
_____
_____
_____
_____
_____
_____
_____
_____

_____

_____

_____

_____

_____

_____

_____

_____

_____

_____

_____

_____

_____

_____

_____

_____

_____

_____

_____

_____

_____

_____

_____

_____

_____

"You must plan for success, not hope to get there by chance."

—TOM PLATZ

"Always be a first-rate version of yourself, instead

of a second-rate version of somebody else."

—JUDY GARLAND

_____
_____
_____
_____
_____
_____
_____
_____
_____
_____
_____
_____
_____
_____
_____
_____
_____
_____
_____
_____
_____
_____
_____

_____

_____

_____

_____

_____

_____

_____

_____

_____

_____

_____

_____

_____

_____

_____

_____

_____

_____

_____

_____

_____

_____

"90% of any pain comes from trying to keep the pain a secret."

—ROBERT HOLDEN, PH.D

"Promise me you'll always remember: You're braver
than you believe, and stronger than you seem,
and smarter than you think."

—A.A. MILINE

Be Yourself. No One Else Is Qualified!

My wish is that you keep your completed workbook, as it is a reminder of the hard work you have done thus far and a refresher when new challenges arise. This journey that you are on is very personal, and it is my pleasure to assist you as you step out of old habits and into new ones. I hope **Digging for Goals** continues to provide you with the necessary tools and exercises to chart your Life Course and get beyond those obstacles that have held you back in the past. Here is to your continued bright future…shine on!!

References

I want to thank the many authors who have written books on Leadership, Coaching, Happiness, Gratitude, Meditation, Self-help, Strengths, and Personal Discovery.

I have read hundreds of books on these subjects, and it would be impossible for me to name them all. It is important to note that the wisdom shared from reading these books will be seen reflected in the pages of **Digging for Goals**.

Special thanks go to:

Happy for No Reason by Marci Shimoff: *www.HappyforNoReason.com*

Finish Strong by Dan Green: *www.SimpleTruths.com*

The Calm Technique by Paul Wilson

Be All You Can Be by John C. Maxwell: *www.JohnMaxwellOnLeadership.com*

Developing the Leader Within You by John C. Maxwell

First Things First by Stephen R. Covey

The 7 Habits of Highly Effective People by Stephen R. Covey

All I Really Need To Know I Learned in Kindergarten by Robert Fulghum

Little Gold Book of YES Attitude by Jeffrey Gitomer: *www.gitomer.com*

The Art of Happiness by H.H. The Dalai Lama

Emotional Intelligence by Daniel Goleman

You Already Know How to Be Great by Alan Fine

Do It! Let's Get Off Our Buts by Peter McWilliams

Beat the Clock and Organize your Life by Donald E. Wetmore

Science of Mind Magazine

Mind Tools: *www.mindtools.com*

The Coaching Tools Company: *www.thecoachingtoolscompany.com*

About the Author

Mary Barnes Johnson, PLCC, PCC is a Professional Life Coach trained through the University of Wisconsin's prestigious Professional Life Coaching Certification Program. She is also a Social and Emotional Intelligence Certified Coach through the ISEI. Mary is widely recognized for her exceptional performance as a leader in the jewelry industry. First as a top-seller herself, and then as a Team Leader, coach, and mentor for others, Mary has assisted hundreds of business professionals in overcoming obstacles and attaining personal and career goals. Also a Certified Yoga Instructor, **Digging for Goals** is Mary's first book.

www.diggingforgoals.com

Printed in the United States
By Bookmasters